At Work

Joan McNerney

Contents

Caregiver

Maybe it had been too
much helping her mother.
She hurried home after work
with medicine, carrying bags of
groceries, rushing to cook.
Endless cleaning, piles of wash.
Gloria arranged medical visits,
wrote checks, handled mail,
balanced accounts.

Then there were all the little things.
Turn up the radio. Turn it down.
Run out for candy. Pick up newspapers.
Find something cool to drink.
Make something hot. Every day
her mother's health seemed worse.

Visiting her in the hospital,
Gloria consulted doctors.
Trying to digest complicated
medical terms coiled in
convoluted sentences.
Straining to interpret arched
eyebrows half smiles mumbles.

Everything led to dead ends.
Sorrow stabbed at her with
its blazing knife. Finally
there was nothing left to do
but light candles in church.

Grocery Cashier

After punching in, she opens her
register, counts bills and splits
up rolls of coins. Her arms ache
from yesterday. From pulling together
store items, piling them in bags.

Another day in this dismal place.
Saccharine MUSAC, dim lights
dreary corridors, dingy floors.
No clock, no water fountain,
no public restroom. Aisles stocked
with cans, boxes, frozen foods.

Pushing carts full of packaged meat,
donuts, cases of beer...customers
creep up in line. Trance-like they
press forward with crinkled coupons,
handing out cash or swiping cards.

A camera is poised on her.
Registers are monitored and
the number of sales counted.
Making sure nothing slips by,
"The Man" is always watching.

Hospital Switchboard Operator

After thirty years of service,
Francine knows she hears the
heart beat of this hospital.

Voicemail, call waiting, cell phones
are just gadgets, she speaks for
clinics, ICU's and admissions.

Francine is the one who connects
post surgery status reports to loved ones.
She can sense the tension in their speech.

The weary sick call for visits to clinics.
Others anxiously request test results
be sent to their addresses.

Doctors park in designated spaces.
Walking briskly in a flurry of white jackets,
they converse in their own language.

Francine knew how to listen.

Housewife

No wonder so many women go crazy.

What we do is invisible.
Only a messy house or room
gets any notice. Only a burnt
dinner receives a review.

Who says how wonderful to have
fresh sheets, washed pressed clothes,
healthy delicious meals, refrigerators
cabinets clean and stocked?
Not to mention that spotless bathroom.

And children with all their screeching
demands.   Where are their toys?
How could bad brother do that? Or they
look up at you as if you were some puzzle.
Then his majesty enters surveying his castle.
Can he even fathom how exhausted you are?

No wonder so many women go crazy.

Meteorologist

One summer when only seven,
she heard thunderstorms bursting
through skies, watched lightning
slash bright Z's across night.

Later she studied for hours currents
of mercurial storms and cloud
formations. Stratus, altostratus, cirrus,
cumulus fell swiftly from her lips.

Some places burned with rings of blistering
winds sweeping across the desert. Rains
rammed houses downstream on the plains.
Northern ice bashed trees breaking power lines.

Her desire was to understand grand forces…
tornado, hurricane, drought, blizzard.
Calculating air currents, moisture, heat
or cold indices to predict the atmosphere.

Moods of the sky master puzzled her.
She only knew what she did not know.
Why this same force creates rainbows
yet pummels whole towns with its fists?

Retail Sales Clerk

Janice wore black shoes and clothes
as prescribed by management.

Laughing she called it her uniform
for these last twenty years.

Colors come and go, mustard,
fuchsia, magenta, electric green.

Hems up and down, necklines
dipping or close to the throat.

Some styles were all fuss and
flutter. Others sharp, tailored.

She loved to press her hands
fingering racks of satins, velvets.

Janice watched customers pry into
purses to find charge cards.

"Wear it with smiles" she called as
shoppers wandered downstairs.

Thrift Shop Volunteer

Deborah descends by clutching
a teetering banister to the
bowels of this holy place.

A sign welcomes all to
St. Mary's Basement Boutique
where scent of unloved clothing
floats through the small room.

For one half hour, she will hang
up grubby blouses and skirts.
Then begin straightening
mounds of faded tee shirts
and torn blue jeans.

The men's corner rarely changes.
A few lumpy jackets, old corduroy
slacks and worn sweaters.
Nearby a small rack holds several
ladies night gowns and robes.

There are bright children's
clothes with boxes of plastic toys,
games at the front of the store.

Deborah glances up at the clock as
another afternoon is almost over.
That will be "one dollar"
she says to another parishioner.

It's the smiles from children as she
hands them some peppermint candies
that will be her paycheck for the day.

The Teacher

Had hoped some would leave,
rise above dirty factory gates
past plumes of smoke spewing
from the cement plant.

Occasionally when discussing
great American novels, the walls
shook. Ravines were being blasted
for more rocks to crush into powder.

She wished they would not become
clerks for soul-less chain stores or
cooks in fast food joints where
smells of burning grease lingered.

What was the use of teaching literature
and poetry to these teens who would
soon grow listless? Their spirits ground
down like stones in the quarry.

Waitress

Sally thought everything was
up to luck and she had zero.
Her chances got swept
away with yesterday's trash.

Every day working in this
dumpy dinner slinging hash.

There were the regulars
who knew her name and
left good tips. They had
no place else to go.

Her feet swelled up at
the end of lunch rush.

Sally wiped tables filling
ketchup bottles, salt shakers,
sugar jars while staring out the
window at pulsing rain.

Waiting a half hour for the bus,
winds tangling her hair.

She stopped at the market to
bring a few groceries home.
Struggling now to open her door,
only cold rooms would greet her.

The Receptionist

Has a permanent smile etched
upon her face. Shops at the very
best thrift stores and takes off
those hi-heeled shoes often.

Her gracious manner is dazzling
as Jennifer perpetually waves off
secretaries, clerks, junior executives.

Then a board member enters.
Her shoes slipped on, her hi-heels
click clicking over marbleized floors.

 "Can I get you anything, sir?"
she asks in breathless anticipation.

Word Processor

She often thought words
just spilled through her fingers.
It was all learned so long ago
by touch typing in school.

Then she was thrilled by winning
an over ninety-words-a-minute
prize. Margie was sure to
transcribe important documents.

She finished the form letter. Now what
must be remembered was paragraph
three goes with addressee list five.

Section seven contains financial
disclosure which only went to top list
number one. Someone would check it.

Technological advances had replaced
people. Equipment never felt sick or
required holidays, vacations, breaks.
Much more cost effective.

Margie wanted to close her eyes
against this flood of words. Shut
her ears against the pounding of
machines, sighs of other operators.

Accountant

During the day,
he could calculate
the secrets of ciphers
grabbling with white
ledgers and tight rows
of numbers.

Richard knew how statistical
data can be rigged while
cash flow double entries
could conceal trouble.
His eyes were wary
but he still believed
in good faith credit.

As night grew so did his
appreciation of the
eloquence of one.
That fat place maker
known as zero. Why
mystics marveled
at the holy seven.

While Richard slept his
dreams multiplied.
Suddenly long division
subtracted an unknown
quantity yet sums still
added up. Where had
his equations wandered?

Delivery Guy

Ray comes all winter
with office supplies.
He calls female workers
"gorgeous". Smiles
spread like wild fire.

Besides reams of paper,
ink cartridges, he carries
the sun. Says it fits perfectly
into his bowling bag.

Sprinting upstairs, balancing
boxes of staples, paper clips,
pens, Ray shouts. "I brought
the sun with me today, slung
it right over my shoulder."

He brings all day glow…
what they want on
those icy dark afternoons
to make them
feel sizzling warm.

The History Professor

Sat in dusty corners of a mildew
room fingering old tomes. His
murmurs filling the night as he
thumbed through yellowed pages.

He had tried to weave history into
daily life for his classes, intertwining
 tapestries from the past.

For some students, the scholastic life
was fulfilling but many simply met the
requirements for graduation.

Countless battles had been analyzed
when he was young and fresh,
excited by war and strategy.

Floating through his memory
were dates and places and names.
Yes, the names of the valiant.

Now they were forgotten as he
would soon be. Gone to that
destination none have studied.

The Librarian

Always cherished the sanctity of
this place. This refuge of
knowledge arranged in infallible
logic of the Dewey Decimal system.

Brian loved to touch these volumes.
Especially heavy reference
dictionaries, atlases, almanacs
and encyclopedias. Those sheltered
in secluded shelves for staff only.

Children come along each day
to feast on colorful books. Lounging
in small chairs, they become
spellbound by cornucopias of words.

Mostly he likes the retirees who
linger with newspapers and
magazines in the reading corner.
They confess not to understand
computers, writing down requested titles.

At the end of evening, Brian walks
through the quiet. Before leaving,
he will select a saga of spicy
adventure to flavor his evening.

Long Haul Driver

At first Mike was thrilled by the road
thinking it an adventure to roam
through cities and states.

His truck a massive 18 wheeler
winding through snake-like
overpasses, gleaming in sunlight
across ten lane highways.

But then he had to drive
so many hours arriving
only to wait for the next
work order, inhaling fumes
in the cold and in the heat.

Coffee was not enough
now he needed No Doze…
easy to pick up at gas stops.
But how to deal with the pain
in his legs, arms and neck?

Later he felt a slave to the
choking engine and ugly
concrete. The same signs
everywhere, big box stores,
eating holes and truck stops
with cheap souvenirs.

Weary of this relentless surge
of everything always going
forward and that demanding clock.
Finally Mike felt left behind.

Maintenance Man

Everything falls apart,
all things rot and crack.

Each day another tenant
fills out forms to request
repairs.   Hot water tanks
burst, sinks back up, toilets jam.
Smoke alarms break.
It's a messy life, he pushes
against riptide.

All spring and summer,
weeds keep growing.
Leaves gather during fall.
In winter time, ice
covers walkways.

It's time to go home now.
Tomorrow he will return
to pick up the pieces again.

Pharmacist

George thought of himself as a
modern alchemist. Fluent
in this arcane language.
Knowing the composition within
so many minute capsules.

The rest of the store could
be in a gas station or bargain
store. Filled with candies,
lip sticks, other frivolous items.

If you simply had a cough, syrup
could be found on aisle three.
His area was sacred to patients,
those with serious ailments.

Filling prescriptions navigating
insurance companies, seeking
authorizations. Always aware of
side effects, multiple drug reactions,
possible allergic problems.

Austere yet approachable,
dispensing heroic potions
from his prized domain
as chemical high cleric.

Recently Unemployed

His days marched in place
days like tin soldiers each one
pushing the next aside.

Hurry, hurry before it is too late...
inside a gaping hole to be filled.
More and more of the surface
of his life was covered by dust.

The hallway gave off a musty odor.
Night after night, lights burned.
Busted dreams heaped in boxes.
Black marks covered floors.

One edge of his room spoke to
the other. His fan purred all summer,
basement furnace heaved all winter.
This incessant sigh gathering dust.
Less and less energy to clean up.
His body betrayed him, both his
bones, his breath betrayed him.

Tomorrow will be more newspapers,
further rounds of calls, another day of
trying to get appointments. Another day
visiting crowded employment agencies.
Another day not worth remembering.

Retired

He sat beside the kitchen window
watching snow fall over sycamores
What could he hope for,
some good news brought by mail.
An unexpected call?

His phone rang with reminders
of medical appointments.
No mail ever came but bills
from doctors, clinics, hospitals,
ads, charity appeals.

He had grown accustomed to suffering,
inured to the idea that his life was
without much happiness or success.
Accustomed to pain running along
his back, through his knees, his feet,
shortness of breath, cancers.

Now in retirement, what was really left?
Just bottles of pills to take every day.
Death used to be something he could
brush off. It happened to someone else.
Now it seemed so close, as if it might
come any day from some cold hand.

The Writer

There are always new demands.
Your bio is either wordy, too short
or impersonal. Tell us about
your educational background.
 What of your professional life?

Use only doc or docx extensions
in a readable font 10 or 12 points.
We only accept page makes.

Take a photo holding our magazine
some place interesting. Send a pix
while you're looking out a window.

The first concept is interesting and the
second. Combine these two. Try
pushing your writing to the next level.

Proof read everything. Send a synopsis
of your work. Here are some interview questions,
maximum 700 words, return by week's end.

Friends always want free copies,
people with money are too cheap to buy
books. Reading is like eating vegetables,
something all of us should do.

Wait until you are dead to make it…BUT
sorry, but got to go to my day job,
need some cash now.